CELEBRATE WHO YOU ARE

Celebrate Who You Are

MARION DUCKWORTH

VICTOR BOOKS®

A DIVISION OF SCRIPTURE PRESS PUBLICATIONS INC.
USA CANADA ENGLAND

Most Scripture quotations are from the *Holy Bible, New International Version,* © 1973, 1978, 1984, International Bible Society. Used by permission of Zondervan Bible Publishers. Other Scripture quotations are from (AMP) *The Amplified Bible,* © 1962, 1964 by Zondervan Publishing House; (KJV) *King James Version* of the Bible; and (TLB) *The Living Bible* © 1971 Tyndale House Publishers, Wheaton, Ill.; used by permission.

Recommended Dewey Decimal Classification: 222.11
Suggested Subject Heading: BIBLE, O.T., HISTORICAL BOOKS—GENESIS

Library of Congress Catalog Card Number: 90-70954
ISBN: 0-89693-816-4

    2   3   4   5   6   7   8   9   10 Printing/Year   94   93

VICTOR BOOKS
A division of SP Publications, Inc.
Wheaton, Illinois 60187

CONTENTS

"I've read shelves full of self-help books so I could find peace with myself, and now I'm more confused than ever." Hundreds of women have said words like these to me during my years of Christian ministry. I said them myself about 18 years ago.

These women and I were looking for help because of something that was going on inside us. "I feel as though I'm living with a person I don't even know or like or with whom I feel comfortable. What in the world is wrong and how can I fix it?" Other women say they have never thought through what it means to be a woman, but now feel a strong need to do so.

What we women want are truths that will enable us to understand and accept ourselves as persons. Then we'll be able to shake hands with ourselves, smile, and settle down.

There's one book that gets to the heart of the matter and that's the Bible. In it, our Father whispers our identity to our spirit the way fathers in one African tribe whisper their newborn's name in the baby's ear so the baby will know who he or she is. I've designed this Bible study to help you discover from the Scripture what God has to say on the subject.

Whether you plan to use it as a personal resource or as the basis for a group study, begin by deciding when is the best time during the day for you to work. Have a couple of translations of the Bible and a dictionary handy. Ask God to be your teacher. If you are going to use this guide for group study, consult the section called "Getting Together" for guidelines.

Remember that the Holy Spirit has promised to reveal the truth to every Christian (John 14:26). He'll be present and ready to do that every time you study, so begin with anticipation and prayer.

For learning and growth to take place, though, you'll need to take time enough to reflect on the Scripture passages and questions. The amount will vary, but what's most important is that you work regularly. A goal of one chapter a week is realistic for most women, however. Even after you close the book and go into your day, you can keep

8

reflecting on a significant verse or key thought.

Who God Says You Are takes you into the Scripture and enables you to discover for yourself what it says about your identity, worth, and purpose. Keep remembering that what the Bible says on the subject is the real truth because it comes from God.

Meet Your Real Self amplifies the theme and shows how factors in today's society and your own experiences play a profound role in the formation of your identity. It also offers suggestions on how to cope with those factors and emphasizes a key truth for personal growth.

The thought questions and exercises in *Build Your Own Identity* will help you build an image in your mind of who you, as an individual, really are. Think of it as a "Celebrating Who I Am" album in which you put word pictures instead of photographs. Sometimes you'll examine old ideas about yourself. Some may not conform to God's explanation of who you are, and you'll learn ways to change your self-image so it is consistent with the truth.

Learning to see yourself through God's eyes is a prerequisite to all other Christian growth. I can personally testify to the life-changing results it produces.

 YOUR CREATION

❧ WHO GOD SAYS YOU ARE ❧

1. Imagine you're handing a salesclerk the check you've just written to pay for your purchase. She asks for two pieces of identification. What will you give her and what kind of information does each provide?

2. Now imagine yourself at a newcomers' party. The hostess leads everyone in a mixer in which you have to tell who you are in 15 seconds. What will you say?

3. Do you find the above ways of identifying yourself unsatisfactory? If so, why?

4. Complete the following statements. Do they more nearly tell who you are?

   I am happiest when

   My favorite time of day is

   My most positive personality characteristic is

   One of my personality flaws is

   One thing I want most is

5. What is the most predominant theory about the origin of human beings that you hear about on TV, in the movies, and in secular literature? How does the Bible contradict that philosophy? Read Genesis 1–2. What title would you give to each of these two chapters?

6. How many times are the words *create, make,* or similar verbs used in 1:26-27? Why do you think the author uses these words so often?

7. What else do you learn about your origin from the following verses?

   Job 33:4

   Psalm 119:73

   Isaiah 64:8

8. Reread Genesis 1:26-30 for a fresh perspective, substituting your own name and the personal pronoun *I* for "man," "male and female," and "you." What words describe how that makes you feel?

9. Write a newspaper headline for this event.

10. What is the process God used to create Adam in 2:7? To create Eve in 2:21-22? Does 2:20 give a clue as to why He used a different process for each? Explain your answer.

11. Compare Adam's creation in 2:7 to that of Eve in 2:20-21. Is one more miraculous than the other? State reasons for your conclusion.

12. Perhaps Eve's beginning does seem wondrous to you, but your own doesn't. The process of continuous creation through the human reproductive process may seem purely a human function. What new view on the subject do you get from reflecting on Eve's words in Genesis 4:1-2?

13. Reflect on what you know about the biological process in which sperm and ovum unite and a fetus is formed, and on the fact that it was God who created that process. Put your thoughts into words.

14. Read Psalm 139:15-16 and list five facts about your own creation that reinforce the idea that it was a miracle too. Notice that in Psalm 139:14, the psalmist praises God for the miracle of *his* creation. Use your own words to do the same thing.

15. As a woman, you are part of the larger species called *mankind.* Read Genesis 1:26 where that word is used. *The Amplified Bible* puts it this way: "God said, Let Us [Father, Son, and Holy Spirit] make mankind in Our image, after Our likeness"; so as a woman, you belong to the race called _____ that was created in two sexes.

16. As a result, everywhere in Scripture where statements or promises are made or instructions given to *man* meaning "mankind," they

refer to both sexes. In the following examples, what statements, instructions, or promises apply to you?

Psalm 1:1

Matthew 4:4

Matthew 12:35-36

John 2:25

17. Because God is our Creator, what attitudes do the following Scriptures suggest we are to have toward Him?

Nehemiah 9:6

Psalm 33:6-9

Psalm 95:1-7

Psalm 121

Isaiah 40:28-31

❦ *MEET YOUR REAL SELF* ❦

Perhaps you've wondered if the preoccupation with personal identity emphasized in *Celebrate Who You Are* is self-centered. Aren't Christians supposed to stop thinking about themselves?

It depends on how and why you're preoccupied. There's a big difference between thinking *selfishly* (being overly occupied with self-interest, which is condemned in Scripture) and *self-identity* (knowing who you are, which is not condemned in Scripture).

As the only creatures who have self-consciousness, or a sense of their own existence, it's natural for us to want to know who we are. It's a built-in desire. And more of us are searching for answers today because we live in a society that has lost its sense of origin.

The widespread acceptance of evolution and the subsequent belief that we are only a highly developed animal whose life has no real meaning, is a foremost reason for that. That may not be what *we* believe; still we are continuously exposed to the teaching, and it has a very subtle effect.

Society has always been ready to tell us who we are. Once, the guidelines were simple: if a woman was born into a peasant family, she was a peasant. From the church, which was the central voice in the community, she received the rest of the information regarding her origin and purpose.

But since the industrial revolution and the secularization of the Western world, one's identity has been blurred. As women, we've been caught in the middle of violent social change over what it means to be a woman and how we are to live out our lives. That's why it's urgent for each one of us personally to go back to the Word of God and see for ourselves who God says we are.

Unquestionably, the first thing that we see is that we are His creation. Each of us is a miracle from the hand of God, continuously reproduced through the plan He designed. While the disbelief of society and its debasement of the sexual process may have tarnished the image of sexual reproduction, it can never change the truth that it is from the mind of God Himself.

Jesus Christ certainly had a solid grasp of His identity. He knew where He came from—that He was the divine Son of God, preexistent and eternal. But He also described Himself as the Son of Man—a human being—part of mankind and the male of the species. In addition, He had some very definite personal characteristics that made Him unique from every other Israelite living in Palestine then.

Jesus Christ knew who He was. His identity differs from ours, of course, because He was God incarnate and we are not. Man's opinion couldn't change His firm conviction. That's a goal for which we all can strive.

The same Scripture that tells us who Jesus Christ is tells us who we are: creatures created in God's image, female gender, individuals who are members of the race called *mankind.*

Psalm 100:1-3 is a celebration of joy to God because these things are true.

> Shout for joy to the Lord,
> all the earth.
> Worship the Lord with gladness;
> come before Him with joyful songs.
> Know that the Lord is God.
> It is He who made us, and we are His;
> we are His people, the sheep of His pasture.

Now, that's something to shout about!

❧ *BUILD YOUR OWN IDENTITY* ❧

This part of the study will help you develop a "Celebrating Who I Am" album. The activities and questions are designed to help you internalize your true, biblical identity.

1. For the first entry in your album of who you are, write down what you know about your own birth. Now, write a statement that sums up your origin as described in Genesis 1–2. Read your statement over and let it sink in that this is part of your identity.

2. Perhaps you've never seen yourself as a miraculous creation before. Reflect on Psalm 139:13-16 and let the words communicate that fact to you. Memorize that passage in the translation that has the most meaning for you. If you already know it, reflect on it again. Since the words are a prayer, say them to God from your own inner woman. Emphasize the personal pronouns *you* and *your* as you do so.

3. Each day this week, list one part of your body that "is fearfully and wonderfully made" (Psalm 139:14). What about each body part makes it so miraculous?

4. Draw a picture of yourself as a fetus in your mother's womb — the kind of picture you might make if you were a child. Indicate the fact that God is engineering your formation and sees your development.

5. Imagine you've decided to give a party so you and your women friends can celebrate the wonder of your creation. What Scripture verses would you use as a theme? What songs would you sing? What kinds of decorations and colors would signify the way you feel? Each person has to fill out a name tag telling the truth they most want people to know about them. What will your tag say?

CHAPTER TWO

Celebrate YOUR RE·CREATION

❦ *WHO GOD SAYS YOU ARE* ❦

1. You have been chosen for a beauty make-over by experts. What would you ask them to do for you?

2. These changes have been external. But suppose you could be made over inside. What would you ask for?

3. Immediately after Eve was created, do you think she needed a make-over? Or was she physically perfect? Explain your reasoning.

4. When God created life, how did He describe it? See Genesis 1:12, 21, 25. What word did He use?

5. What phrase in 1:31 shows that description includes mankind as well?

6. Look up that key word in the dictionary. Which definition most applies here?

7. In your opinion, why does that description of creation fit perfectly?

8. In Genesis 3, the first of two important dramas unfolds. This one is titled "Mankind's Disobedience." Read Genesis 3:1-7 to see the scenario. What is the identity of the serpent? See Revelation 12:9.

9. How would you describe the serpent from the information given in the following passages?

   Genesis 3:1, 4

   Matthew 4:3

   John 8:44

   1 Peter 5:8

10. Imagine that you are Eve—freshly created in a world you've just begun to explore. What words describe you? Do you think these qualities influenced Satan to tempt Eve and not Adam? Although

Eve was the one who ate the fruit first, why was Adam also guilty? See Genesis 2:15-17.

11. Was God's command restated accurately in Genesis 3:2-5? Read Genesis 2:15-17 and describe what you'd say if the serpent were testifying on the witness stand and you were cross-examining him.

12. What are the three ways in Genesis 3:6 that Eve was tempted? Exactly what was it that the serpent offered Eve?

13. Reread Genesis 2:16–3:5. Then look up the word *knowledge* in the dictionary. The definition that most applies is

14. Describe the first couple's inner state before they ate the fruit and afterward. What insight do you get from 1 John 2:16? If you had been Eve, what would you have written in your journal about the preceding experience?

15. What two words in Isaiah 43:27 describe the first couple's act?

16. If you were Eve, what kind of make-over would you have liked now?

17. How did Adam and Eve's act affect their relationship with God? See Genesis 3:8-10.

18. In the midst of this unhappy scene, God plants the first of a series of clues indicating that He will take restorative measures. It is found in Genesis 3:15. Write in your own words what He promises. Refer to more than one translation. Next to the following passages, describe other clues God gave as well.

   Isaiah 7:14

   Isaiah 11:1-3

   Micah 5:2

   Zechariah 14:9

19. Focus now on the second drama that unfolds in the New Testament. Its title is "Mankind's Restoration and Re-creation." The most important players are described in Hebrews 9:13-14. Who are they?

20

20. When does Galatians 4:4 say that God interceded for mankind's restoration? Who accomplished it? What word describes what God did for man? Use a dictionary or another translation to find the meaning of words that are unclear.

21. What act makes mankind's restoration possible? See 1 Corinthians 15:3-4.

22. A friend has asked you to explain the steps one must take in order to be restored to fellowship with God and to be spiritually re-created. Consult the following passages and write out what you'd say.

Acts 3:19, Acts 4:12, John 3:3, John 1:12, and Romans 10:9-10

23. Your friend has taken those steps. Now she wants to understand more completely what just took place. Using the following passages as a guide, describe what you'd tell her.

Acts 2:38

Romans 8:9

1 Thessalonians 5:9-10

Titus 3:5-7

24. What does the Apostle Paul have to say about his own rebirth in 1 Timothy 1:15-16?

25. Read Paul's exclamation of praise for the miracle of his rebirth in 1 Timothy 1:17. Read it again, and if you have experienced rebirth, speak it to God as a personal exclamation of praise. Then put the verse in your own words, writing it here, and reflecting on what you've written.

❦ *MEET YOUR REAL SELF* ❦

For years, every time I read what the Apostle Paul wrote about the new birth in 2 Corinthians 5:17, I felt guilty. "Therefore, if any man be in Christ, he is a new creature; old things are passed away; behold, all things are become new." (KJV) *I* was "in Christ" because I had received Him into my life, so I was a new creature. Then why wasn't I completely transformed, with shiny, new habits? Why was I behaving in many ways like the old model?

Like most other people, at the moment of rebirth I didn't understand all the theological implications any more than I understood all the biological inner workings when my husband Jack and I conceived our first child. But at the confirmation of physical conception and the moment of spiritual rebirth, I rejoiced and felt as though a permanent smile had settled inside me.

When I became a Christian, however, I was aware of one very significant thing. Instead of knowing *about* God the way I had before—that He was the Divine Being who existed in a place called "heaven"—I knew that I knew Him. Now when I prayed, I knew He heard me.

The difference was in relationship. I know now that's exactly what the Apostle Paul was emphasizing in 2 Corinthians 5. "God . . . reconciled us to Himself" (v. 18).

The word *reconciled* means "to make friendly again." Or, as *The Amplified Bible* puts it, "brought us into harmony with Himself." The "old things" that have passed away in verse 17 are separation from God and the necessity of punishment for sin, since Christ brought us together and paid for our disobedience with His death.

The intimacy between God and man that existed at the first flush of creation has been restored. And intimacy certainly did exist then.

What could be more intimate than walking with God in the cool of the evening? But after mankind's sin, all that ended. The couple was banished from the Garden. It took the blood from the wounds of God's own

Son to make payment and reunite us in friendship again.

That moment we also became part of a new creation (a phrase that is an alternate reading for "new creature" in 1 Corinthians 5:17). Instead of merely being a member of a race called "mankind," at the moment of reconciliation we actually become members of the kingdom of God.

So if the creation account in Genesis is a miracle to make us gasp in awe, how much more must the Holy Spirit-engineered re-creation impact us. The former—visible and tangible as it was—boggles the mind. But our wonder over the latter—invisible, intangible, and spiritual—is a breath drawn inward that never ends. Women who have been Christians for a while, however, may find the newness has worn off, like a gift taken for granted. Perhaps Peter anticipated that when he wrote his first letter.

Take a second look, he seems to urge. *Reflect deeply on the wonder of what you see.* Hear Him speak the words with the love and conviction of one who came early to the empty tomb. "You have been regenerated—born again—not from a mortal origin (seed, sperm) but from one that is immortal by the *ever* living and lasting Word of God" (1 Peter 1:23, AMP). *Miracle* he calls the new birth as he writes to the centuries. Lay it side by side with the physical birth, he urges, when sperm and ovum united, followed by gestation and a squalling "us." See with your inner eyes. As we think and worship, we begin to sense afresh the wonder of our rebirth. The Creator actually implanted in us another kind of seed—the essence of His own Life—and we were made new.

I have finally come to understand what Paul meant when he said I was a "new creature." First, he was describing my position before God: a member of His eternal kingdom—clean and forgiven—because God has ascribed to me the righteousness of Jesus Christ. Second, Paul was also describing my relationship to him—reconciled and living as intimates.

I also know now what re-creation is not. It is not a Cinderella story in which God plays the role of fairy godmother and zaps us with His wand, transforming us into princesses. I know now that's as foolish as expecting that, at the moment of physical birth, a baby will be fully developed with teeth and the ability to use language.

Wanting to mature in Christ is good. Neurotic preoccupation to "get all growed up" is not. It keeps us from focusing our attention on God and cultivating a deepened friendship, which is the very thing new birth is all about. Besides, it's that relationship out of which maturity grows.

No matter how long ago we were reborn, we can keep our wonder fresh. One way is by breathing our thanks to God every time we confess a sin and accept forgiveness; every time He illuminates a new truth in Scripture; every time we talk over a problem with Him. *Thank You, Father, for all You've done so that we can be friends.*

🦋 BUILD YOUR OWN IDENTITY 🦋

To discover more about your true, biblical identity, continue developing your "Celebrating Who I Am" album.

1. Write your rebirth announcement as though you were sending it to friends. You may not know the exact date, but be sure to include your name, your Father's name, and other pertinent details of the occasion.
2. If you haven't been reborn, you can do so now. First, review question 22 under *Who God Says You Are*. Then pray, asking God to forgive your sins. Invite Jesus Christ into your life. If you have done that, write your own rebirth announcement following the guidelines of question 1. Then review question 15.
3. Memorize a verse you don't know yet from *Who God Says You Are*, questions 22 or 23. Emphasize key words in your mind as you do so. Why are they especially significant to you? Tell God your thoughts.
4. Each day this week, reflect on and write your response to one aspect of your recreation by God:
   a. forgiven
   b. eternal life instead of death
   c. member of the Kingdom of God
   d. redeemed
   e. know God
   f. indwelled with the Holy Spirit
5. Plan to celebrate your rebirthday each year. Choose a date if you don't know when it took place. Write it on your calendar. Enter it on your list of birthdays. How will you commemorate the occasion? To what ministry will you give a gift of appreciation to God? On what Scripture will you reflect? If you already celebrate your rebirthday, what new things would you like to do on that occasion?

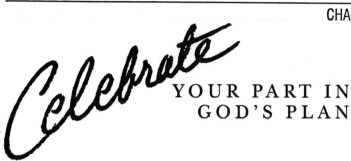

CHAPTER THREE

YOUR PART IN
GOD'S PLAN

❧ WHO GOD SAYS YOU ARE ❧

1. Think of a female TV character or fictional character you admire. How does she spend her time? Does she have a job outside the home? What do you like/dislike about the way she does her jobs?

2. Look through ads and illustrations in women's magazines and note the implications they make about women and work. What image do they present?

3. Compare career opportunities that existed for your mother and grandmother to ones that exist for women today. Describe some differences.

4. What evidence do you see in Genesis 2:15 that part of mankind's function was to work?

5. What did God say was one role or function that mankind was to fill? See Genesis 1:26 and 9:2. How do you know from Genesis 1:27 that this applies to females too? Does Psalm 8:6-8 give you more insight

into the subject? What are the key words and phrases and their synonyms in each of these passages?

6. How has mankind's fall into sin interfered with his fulfilling the responsibility described in the previous question? What evidence of that failure do you see today?

7. In Genesis 3:16, what is one specific function that God said Eve—and by implication—womankind would fill?

8. According to Genesis 9:1, 7, why did God call women to be mothers? In what ways is this role one women are to carry out in union with their husbands? Give reasons for your answer.

9. While Eve was the one who would primarily take care of home and family, what was man's work? See Genesis 3:19.

10. Many think the Bible gives a narrow view of a woman's role. How does Proverbs 31:10-31 disprove that? What responsibilities other than housework and childcare are described?

11. In the following passages, what other roles did women fill?

Genesis 29:9

Judges 4:4

Ruth 2:2-3a

Esther

12. A woman's responsibilities change as she goes through life. What new role did Eve take on in Genesis 4:17?

13. It didn't take long for mankind to identify himself by the work that he did. What evidence of that do you see in Genesis 4:20-22?

14. Later, those in positions of greater power took advantage of those in positions of lesser power. Describe how that happened in Exodus 1:6-14.

15. Because of God's command to repopulate the earth, Jewish women saw their most honored role as motherhood. Those who could bear children were honored; those who couldn't, therefore, were looked down on. How is Sarai's desperation revealed in Genesis 16:1-4? What word is used to describe Hagar's attitude toward Sarai?

16. The story of another such woman is told in 1 Samuel 1:1-20. Read it and write about it as though you were telling it to a friend. Especially emphasize her feelings about being childless. Include the following information: Why was Hannah barren? What circumstances made it worse? How long did she have to endure it? How did she finally come to feel? How would you describe her prayer to God? How was she misunderstood and why? What was the outcome of the situation?

17. Gaining the most important roles in society became the primary goal for many individuals through the centuries because that was the way they gained identity. Jesus demonstrated a completely different attitude toward work. What word in Philippians 2:5-7 describes it? How does the incident in John 13:1-5 demonstrate His attitude? What words in verse 3 make Him the ultimate role model?

18. Our roles in life are not meant to give us status. The principle we are to keep in mind instead is described in Ephesians 6:7. Write it in your own words.

19. That principle turns what could be drudgery into a privilege. Imagine you are the slaves and masters described in Ephesians 6:5-6, 9. Write a personal code of behavior based on the verses.

20. What further impetus to work biblically do you see in Ephesians 6:8?

🍂 *MEET YOUR REAL SELF* 🍂

My family and I had just moved to the city where I now live. The first Sunday found my husband and me seated in the Pastor's Welcome Class in a neighborhood church. Each person present was instructed to give his or her name and tell something about himself or herself. When it was my turn, I described myself this way: "My husband and I just resigned after spending nearly 11 years as home missionaries."

As soon as the words left my mouth, I gasped silently. *I wasn't a home missionary anymore. Who was I now?*

I wasn't the only woman in the room who was identifying herself by her roles. "I'm a secretary in the State Legislature," and "I'm a nurse," I heard other women say.

Of course we identify ourselves by our roles. Why not? Isn't that the message society has been sending us for years? Haven't they continuously emphasized the importance of "becoming somebody" by filling important roles. Like scientist, surgeon, or fashion designer?

Not only that, but women-of-the-year are multi-roled. Surgeons *and* wives *and* mothers *and* organization chairpersons. Certainly, they are not "just housewives."

Is it any wonder that we finally come to equate what we do with who we are? Like so many others, I'd fallen into the "I am what I do" trap. First, it was radio operator, then wife, then mother, then home missionary.

The day came (thankfully, I know now), when I ran out of roles by which to identify myself. As a result, I was forced by God to learn to identify myself not by what I did, but by who I am.

Women have admitted to me—sometimes tearfully—that for years they've been doing what I did. One sat across from me at a retreat I led. "I was the oldest in the family. It was my responsibility to be a substitute 'mommy' because both of my parents worked in a business. I grew up thinking that filling roles justified my existence."

Another woman said, "The most important thing to my dad was for his children to be a success in business. So that became my goal, because I wanted to please my father. Eventually, my career became my identity."

Both of these women as well as I myself finally learned that we were created, not to *do* but to *be*. That's what Jesus intimated when He gave the greatest commandment: "Love the Lord your God with all your heart and with all your soul and with all your mind and with all your strength" (Mark 12:30).

So a truly successful woman is one whose primary goal is to live from moment to moment in intimacy with God. Her reason for living is not to *do* but to *be*.

The more she pursues intimacy with God, the more she discovers that her motivation to fill her roles joyfully grows out of being with Him. That's one of the reasons Jesus Christ could live such a *giving* kind of life. His motivation to do His work on earth grew out of His intimacy with His Father. Working to build status is to be as foreign to us as it was to Him.

We must allow no one to press us to believe any differently about what we do. Jesus forever slashed through the world's concepts of work when He elevated the tiniest service that is done out of love for Him. "If anyone gives even a cup of cold water to one of these little ones because he is My disciple, I tell you the truth, he will certainly not lose his reward" (Matthew 10:42).

How do we become free from the tyranny of roles as status? By making experiential intimacy with God our primary goal. By learning to *be* with Him as we chauffeur kids, lead board meetings, and clean out the refrigerator. It's by living with Him and in Him that we learn to see our roles as opportunities to serve. Not only that, but we'll learn to see them as opportunities to become servants through to the core in the same way that Jesus (our role model) was.

❧ *BUILD YOUR OWN IDENTITY* ❧

Continue developing your "Celebrating Who I Am" album.

1. List five of your primary responsibilities. Rate yourself in each on a scale of 1–10 according to the following criteria: wholeheartedness; sincerity; done out of love generated by intimacy with God. Ask God to gradually enable you to do them more joyfully because they are a way to show your love for Him. Expect Him to help you do that, day by day.

2. Memorize Ephesians 6:7-8. Before you do, read it in a second translation. During the memorization process, read it several times slowly, each time emphasizing a key word and see what new insights you receive.

3. Every day this week, evaluate the way you performed your tasks by asking yourself the following questions: Have I been resentful at times. If so, when and why? Do I have a realistic view of my capacity? Am I trying to be a superwoman to prove something to myself or someone else? Have I failed to carry out some responsibility? If so, why? Have I seen my roles as a way to achieve identity or as a way to serve God? Am I working out of love or duty? What changes do I need to make?

4. One of woman's roles is to take dominion — or to be a ruler — over the earth because she is God's representative. Read the newspaper this week and look for ways you may be able to do that, like caring for the environment or protecting an endangered species of animal. Ask God to show you one area in which you can help.

5. Celebrate your opportunity to serve God through the responsibilities He's given you. Do it by writing notes, making phone calls, or saying a personal word to people for whom you perform tasks, such as your employer, family, church representative, or community organization. Keep Ephesians 6:5-9 in mind as you determine what you can say to them that expresses the spirit of that passage.

CHAPTER FOUR

Celebrate YOUR INESTIMABLE WORTH

❧ WHO GOD SAYS YOU ARE ❧

1. What three items in your home do you consider among the most valuable?

2. Is their worth to you based on more than a dollar value? If so, explain why that's true.

3. Suppose you were required to write out a sentence describing your own value as a person. What kinds of things would you take into consideration? Write in a sentence the conclusions you would come to about your worth.

4. Tell a little about an item that has special significance to you because you made it. How would you feel if someone disparages it?

5. God the Father values mankind supremely, but suppose you had no personal knowledge of that fact. Explore the following passages so you can draw conclusions for yourself.

Genesis 1:26-27; 5:1; 28:15

Isaiah 41:10; 46:4

Zechariah 3:17

Romans 5:5-8

These passages show that mankind is of unique importance to God. Think about your own feelings toward something you made. Does that help your understanding? Write your thoughts.

6. Why do you think belief in the theory of evolution as opposed to the Creation account devalues man?

7. What did God do to man in Genesis 1:28a and 9:1a? Look up the key word in the dictionary. What does that tell about His attitude toward human beings?

8. What do Psalm 8:3-5 and Hebrews 2:6-8 say is man's position in the universe? Compare your attitude about this with David's in Psalm 8.

   David's attitude:

My attitude:

9. How do God's actions to preserve mankind in the following passages reveal His attitude toward the human race?

Genesis 7:1-4

Genesis 18:20-33

Exodus 3:7-10

10. What is your conclusion about the Creator's value of mankind from questions 4–9?

11. Imagine that you've been told that the second way we know God rates mankind so highly is through the life of Jesus Christ. Investigate the following and decide how the passages prove that statement to be true.

His birth, Matthew 1:20-21

His life, Isaiah 61:1 and Hebrews 1:1-3

His death, Isaiah 53:3-5

12. In Jesus' day, women were looked down upon. They were subordinate to men and generally didn't speak out in public. The Son of God, however, revealed a very different viewpoint. How do the following incidents show that to be true?

Matthew 8:14-15

Matthew 15:21-28

Luke 10:38-41; John 11:5

John 4:1-26

John 20:1-18

13. What is your conclusion about Jesus' value of mankind and womankind from questions 11–12?

14. A third way God emphasizes how highly He values us is in the New Testament letters He inspired His followers to write. One example is the opening passages of the Apostle Paul's letter to the Ephesians. Analyze what Paul says by reading the appropriate verse, imagining that God is speaking to you, and completing the following statements:

(1:3) Because you are of inestimable worth to Me

(1:4) Before the creation of the world, I wanted you to be with Me through eternity, so

(1:5) It was My pleasure and will to

(1:6-7) I have freely given you

(1:7-8) But that's not all. I also gifted you with

(1:9) Another way I proved your importance to Me is that I

(1:13-14) Finally, I marked you as My own by giving you

15. List the words and phrases in Ephesians 1 that personally impress you regarding how priceless you are to Him.

16. What is your conclusion about the value God places on you from these verses?

17. Perhaps you can believe that God values the human race in general, but still have trouble believing that He values you as an individual. Gideon felt that way. He lived at a time when the Midianites had ravaged Israel and they were struggling just to get food. Read Judges 6:11-16. How did the angel address Gideon? How did Gideon see himself? If you sometimes feel about yourself the way Gideon did, it may help you to notice how the angel dealt with that man's self-doubt. See also Galatians 2:20. Based on that passage, what is God's message to you?

18. The Bible is full of accounts when God showed the importance He places on the individual by the way He helped him or her. Look back over passages in this session for examples and describe them below. Also consult the following passages.

    Joseph in prison (Genesis 39:20-21)

    A sick woman (Matthew 9:20-22)

    Thief on the cross (Luke 23:40-43)

19. What is your conclusion about the value God places on you as an individual?

20. Review this session and based on your own conclusions, revise or add to your answer to question 3.

❧ *MEET YOUR REAL SELF* ❧

Part of my job when I worked in a retail store was to price items for sale. To decide what to charge for a kind of tea or crackers or cheese that we'd never stocked before, did I go to other employees and ask, "How much do you think this should sell for?" Or deliberate with myself: "Let's see. Maybe $1.95?"

Hardly. Instead, I went immediately to the price book. Listed there were the amounts to charge for every product we carried. That book's words were absolute. No arguing.

But when it came to establishing my own worth, instead of going to the Book and accepting what God said there—that humans are invaluable—I listened to other voices. And those other voices said I was a reject.

So I devalued myself. And I'm not the only one who's done that. Nearly every time I speak, women tell me they've done the same thing.

Glenda is one of them. Diagnosed as having cranial stenosis, a condition in which the soft spot in an infant's skull closes prematurely, she experienced impaired coordination and cognitive function as a result. Even after corrective surgery, she was left years behind academically. Besides that, her parents demonstrated significant resentment toward her because of her condition and continually put her down.

About mid-life, Glenda accepted Jesus Christ into her life. Now, the Book inspired by God was the only place to which she was to go to set her worth. But Glenda and I and countless other women who have spent a long time supposing the cut-rate price tags society hangs on us are accurate, need help to believe the truth about ourselves.

That help is available to each of us from the Holy Spirit. He was the One who continually reminded me (when I reverted to believing my old self-concept) of my real worth to God and encouraged me to believe Him instead. *I am the only One who has the authority to tell you who you are. That you are chosen to be My very own. That you are made holy in My eyes so you can spend eternity with Me.*

One of the passages that awed me most and indelibly impressed my identity on my soul was this one: "I want you to realize that God has been made rich because we who are Christ's have been given to Him!" (Ephesians 1:18, TLB) Another translation said that I was God's inheritance!

I thought of my mother's words to me before she died. "I don't have anything of material value to leave you. What I do leave you is this." Then she held up the Bible in her lap. "It's what means the most to me."

That's what an inheritance is: the giver's most valuable possession. And God said in His Word that He has been made rich because I— and other Christians—have been given to Him.

What we need is to be able to internalize our biblical identity so it can motivate the way we live. Here are some ways I've learned to do that:

1. Reflect regularly on portions of Scripture that state God's value of me so that it becomes my mindset.
2. Forgive those who have devalued me. Forgive myself too when I fail to live up to my expectations.
3. Associate with people who confirm my worth so that they can reinforce the truth in me.
4. Develop a biblical image of who God is. Mine may be distorted and keep me from closeness to Him. Keep learning to focus on Him and not myself.
5. Cooperate with God when He provides opportunities to live out my biblical image. Let God set the pace, not my old self.

Sure we're flawed. But flawed or not, God values us highly. He proved it irrefutably when He set the price for our salvation.

It's true. It's in the Book.

🦋 *BUILD YOUR OWN IDENTITY* 🦋

Continue developing your "Celebrating Who I Am" album.
1. Describe one time when your self-worth plummeted. Why did it happen? What new information do you have now that can change your perspective?
2. Think about the special instructions the manufacturer provided with an item you purchased. Suppose God included those kinds of instructions when He re-created you. "You are a very valuable person. Here's how I want you to care for yourself." What are some tips about your personal care that He might have included? Check yourself to see if you value yourself highly enough to care for yourself that way. What conclusions do you come to?
3. Every day this week, write a segment of Ephesians 1:3-14 in your own words. Use other translations to give you insight. Use personal pronouns (*I* and *me* instead of *you* and *we*). Each day, prayerfully reflect on what you've written. What new truths do you see?
   Day 1   (vv. 2-3)
   Day 2   (vv. 4-6)
   Day 3   (vv. 7-8)
   Day 4   (vv. 9-10)
   Day 5   (vv. 11-12)
   Day 6   (vv. 13-14)
4. Memorize the part of Ephesians 1:3-14 that means the most to you.
5. Celebrate your worth by writing a letter to the One who gave you worth. Include worship thoughts and gratitude for His sacrifice of Christ so you could become His inheritance. Include also your honest feelings about your real estimation of yourself. Ask God to help you in whatever ways you need to learn to live by your biblical identity.

CHAPTER FIVE

GOD'S LOVE

❧ *WHO GOD SAYS YOU ARE* ❧

1. Describe the first time you recall someone telling you he or she loved you.

2. What is one way someone significant in your life showed you that he or she loved you? What effect did it have on you?

3. Describe one time you expected love to be demonstrated but it wasn't and the impact that had on you.

4. Although God didn't say "I love you" to Adam and Eve, He did demonstrate His love. How many ways did God express His love in Genesis 2–3?

5. *Love* is one of the most often used words in the English language. To see whether or not it's a central theme in the Bible, look up *love* and its derivatives in a Bible concordance. Is it used often, very often, or rarely? Read the various definitions of love in the dictio-

nary. Compare them to the words for love most often used in the Bible.

phileo — tender affection

agape — unconditional, self-sacrificial concern motivated by the inestimable value of the object.

In what ways does God's love differ from human love?

6. God declares His love for us in the Bible. The first way He does this is by inspiring the writers to explain that love is His basic nature. Look up the following Scriptures and in your own words, write statements that express God's nature of love.

Deuteronomy 10:14-15

Psalm 145:8

Malachi 1:2

John 16:27

1 John 4:16

7. Bible writers go on to describe the characteristics of God's love for *us*. Read the following Scriptures and record words that represent God's love for us.

Deuteronomy 4:31

Psalm 103:8

Jeremiah 31:3

Ephesians 2:4

Since God is the origin of love, the description in 1 Corinthians 13:4-8 applies to Him. Write additional words found here that describe God's love.

8. Based on what you've learned so far, write in your own words a magazine advertisement describing God's love.

9. The second way the Bible teaches us about God's love is by pointing out ways He's demonstrated it. Fill in the following chart.

The passage   The action

Isaiah 63:7-9

John 15:15

Romans 5:8

Hebrews 4:16

James 1:5

2 Peter 3:9

10. John 3:16 is the one verse describing God's love with which we're most familiar. Reflect on the fact that it is God who initiated love, that you are the object of His love, and that He demonstrated His love in so sacrificial a way. If you were going to write a song lyric, what line would you include to communicate your thoughts?

11. The third way the Scripture teaches about God's love is by showing us that He loves individuals. Read the passage listed below. Next to each tell why the verse applies to you.

2 Samuel 12:24-25

John 3:16

John 11:25

John 14:21

Romans 1:7

1 John 4:15

Revelation 22:17

12. God also specifically demonstrated His love for women. What action in the following passages demonstrates that?

Mark 14:1-9

Luke 13:10-13

John 4:1-26

John 19:25-27

13. A fourth way we learn about God's love is through His willingness to be a Father to us. How many times does He use the word *Father* in Matthew 6:5-15 to impress us with our relationship to Him if we are Christians? What specific evidence do you find in 2 Corinthians 6:18 that He includes women?

What further insight about God's fatherhood of you do you learn from these verses?

Psalm 68:5

Isaiah 64:8

Matthew 6:8

Matthew 7:7-11

James 1:17

14. The fifth way God says "I love you" is often harder to understand and accept. Examine Hebrews 12:6. What explanation does God give here and in 1 Peter 1:6-9 of this action as part of His love?

15. A sixth way God impresses us with His love is by the names He calls Himself, because in Scripture a name describes something about the person. Find the name for Christ in each of the following Scriptures. Next to each one, write what it tells you about Christ's love.

Isaiah 9:6

Matthew 1:23

John 1:29

John 10:11

John 15:5

16. Write a word picture of Jesus Christ based on these names.

17. We can tell whether or not someone really cares for us by the names they call us. That's a seventh way we know God loves us. List the ones He uses here.

    Romans 8:17

    1 Peter 2:9

    1 John 3:1

18. Psalmists expressed their love back to God because they were convinced He loved them. What reasons do they give?

    Psalm 59:17

    Psalm 89:1-2

Psalm 100

Psalm 107:1

Psalm 130:7

19. Romans 5:6-8 capsulizes much of what the Bible has to say about God's unselfish love for us. How does it answer your objections that you're too sinful for God to love you? What phrases emphasize the depth of God's love?

20. Write a summary sentence for each of the seven ways God has revealed His love for you in Scripture.

❦ *MEET YOUR REAL SELF* ❦

We should certainly *know* that God loves us. After all, wasn't "Jesus Loves Me" one of the first songs most of us learned to sing? And haven't we heard the slogan, "God loves you," over and over?

The trouble is, "God loves you" has become a cliché—one of those trite sayings with which we are so familiar that it slides across our brains without sinking in. That was certainly true for me. Even though I taught God's love for over a decade to every group from preschool through adult, I didn't believe He meant me.

That's because my subconscious was convinced that I wasn't lovable. So much hearing and repeating made no difference. Other women have confessed the same problem. Diedre, a young artist, blurted out to me, "I can't believe God loves me. How could He? My own mother didn't."

Eileen was 71 years old and recently widowed when she confided, " 'God loves you' are still just words to me."

If I could just feel God's love. Then I could believe it, we think. Feeling loved was a perpetual ache for Mandy because she hadn't experienced it in her human relationships.

"My husband Jerry just doesn't know how to show affection. None of the men in his family are demonstrative." The fact that he was a good provider simply wasn't enough to make her feel loved. Her felt need was for affection, and Jerry wasn't providing that.

The fact that Hilary's father was a good provider wasn't enough for her either. Single and near mid-life, she said, "Always, I've wanted him to put his arms around me and tell me that he loves me. He never has."

God doesn't necessarily meet our felt needs with a quick fix in our emotions. He doesn't necessarily change people in our lives so they'll provide what we need when we need it. But He will enable us to know by experience and with absolute certainty that He—the God of creation—loves us.

Paul puts it this way: "Know—practically, through experience for yourselves—the love of Christ, which far surpasses mere knowledge (without experience)" (Ephesians 3:19, AMP). Know intimately in your inner woman through the inworking of the Holy Spirit with a settledness that it is true. *God does love me.*

How do we begin the process? By internalizing the Scripture regularly through meditation and choosing to act on it. For example: *I choose to believe in Your love. As a result, I'm going to trust You to help me with my felt need—loneliness.*

If, for example, the problem is loneliness, *go* where you'll meet people; *choose* to be friendly; *expect* God to ultimately bring you together with someone to fill your need for human friendship. As a result, you'll *know* God's love through His provision and realize that He really does care about your felt needs.

Even if we feel unlovable, God can help. The first truth we need to assimilate is that His love isn't earned. No valentines from God, no "I love you *because* you're smart/pretty/efficient/successful." He loves us because it's His nature to do so.

We may be fearful, stubborn women; still He loves us. As we begin to trust His love and take the risks we've avoided to protect our egos, we'll find ourselves changing into the women we want to become. Then we'll know it's true: "How great is the love the Father has lavished on us, that we should be called children of God! And that is what we are!" (1 John 3:1)

❧*BUILD YOUR OWN IDENTITY*❧

Continue developing your "Celebrating Who I Am" album.

1. Write your immediate response to the words "God loves you." What do you learn about yourself? Do some "but's" or "in spite of's" come into your mind? "But He can't love me because. . . . " "God loves me in spite of. . . . " Write your thoughts.
2. If you believe God loves you, how will that affect your responses to the following situations?
   ☐ You have to use your grocery money for an unexpected medical expense.
   ☐ You aren't invited to a friend's party.
   ☐ You overhear someone making unkind remarks about you.
3. Memorize the passage from *Meeting Your Real Self* that best communicates God's love for you.
4. Read Psalm 136. Each day this week, write a line of your own, patterned after verses 10-22. Each line should recall one way in which God has demonstrated His love for you personally. Repeat the same refrain after each verse that is used in the original.
5. Celebrate God's love for you by thanking some human being through whom He has expressed His love. Tell the person specifically what he or she has done for you and how it has enriched your life. Then thank God for that person.

CHAPTER SIX

YOUR FEMALENESS

🐚 *WHO GOD SAYS YOU ARE* 🐚

1. What do you like best about being a woman?

2. What do you like least?

3. What does the word *female* mean to you? Consult the dictionary. What new thoughts about femaleness does it give you?

4. Are there times when you feel more feminine than others? What are they?

5. Imagine that your Bible school professor has asked you to speak for five minutes on the subject, "What it means to be a woman." As you go through the passages in this study, record notes for your speech under the sections called "Five-minute Talk."

6. One obvious difference between man and woman is biological. How is Eve's sexuality implied in Genesis 3:16, 20; 4:1?

7. In the Song of Solomon, a poem in which a man and woman express their love for one another, human sexuality is presented as beautiful, and God-given. What words and phrases in the following passages have a romantic or sexual connotation?

5:10-16 (Here, "The Beloved" speaks.)

7:1-9 (These are "The Lover's" words.)

Taken literally, what important attitude toward sexuality do these passages communicate?

8. Five-minute Talk: What would you say in your speech about female sexuality?

9. The female of the species is first called "Eve" in Genesis 3:20. What does that name mean? Reflect on the definition and write down some thoughts it brings to mind.

10. While not every woman is a mother, we can each appreciate the wonder of the process of reproduction and the normal nurturing process. In your own words, tell how each of the following incidents portrays a mother's love.

Genesis 21:8-19

Exodus 1:22–2:4

1 Kings 3:16-27

11. Five-minute Talk: What would you say in your speech about God's gift of motherhood and mother-love to females?

12. What does Adam call the female of the species in Genesis 2:23? In his book *Liberated Traditionalism* (Multnomah Press, p. 112), Professor Ronald A. Allen points out that this word "means the same thing his own name means. His name for her was a happy joke; it was the feminine complement of his own name." Here is Allen's translation of that verse.

> This one! This time!
> (That is, At last—here is one who corresponds directly and truly to me!)
> Bone—from my bones!
> And flesh—from my flesh!
> This one shall be called woman
> For from man this one was taken!

In your own words, describe Adam's feelings the moment the female was presented to him.

13. Five-minute Talk: What would you say in your speech about the name *woman?*

14. The word used in Genesis 2:20 to describe Eve's role is *helper.* Look up the dictionary definition of *helper.* What new light is shed on the role of helper in the following passages? Keep in mind that the word is the same as in Genesis 2:20.

    Psalm 33:20

    Psalm 70:5

    Psalm 115:9

    Psalm 121:1-2

    Who is the person who is to provide the help? If you have seen the role of "helper" as demeaning, how do you see it now?

15. Five-minute Talk: What would you say in your speech regarding woman's role as helper?

16. Examine Galatians 3:26-29 for information on the equality of women. Who is the source of equality? How are we equal? See Colossians

1:12. Look up the dictionary definition of *equal*. Does it help? How?

Five-minute Talk: What would you say in your speech about the equality of women?

17. In Genesis 2:24 God makes a general statement about marriage. Which statement most nearly sums up what He said? Why?

Every woman must marry.

If a woman marries, she and her husband become a new family unit.

18. What reason is given by Jesus in Matthew 19:8-12 for remaining single? Is it for everyone? What reason is given by Paul in 1 Corinthians 7:8, 26-28, 32-35?

19. Examine Ephesians 5:21 to understand the principle of a woman's submission to her husband. How is that principle applied in the following passages?

Ephesians 5:22-23

1 Corinthians 16:15-16

Hebrews 13:17

James 4:7

1 Peter 5:5

Five-minute Talk: In your speech, what conclusions about submission can you draw from the preceding passages?

20. Five-minute Talk: What would you say in your speech about a woman's marital status?

21. The Scriptures describe a woman's femininity in terms of her inner qualities. Which words describe them specifically?

Proverbs 11:16

Proverbs 14:1

1 Timothy 2:9-10

1 Peter 3:1-4

Five-minute Talk: What would you say in your speech about a woman's qualities?

22. Are you ready now to make your "Five-minute Talk"? Review your answers to questions 7, 9, 12, 14, 19 and 21. What three factors about femaleness will you emphasize because they seem most important to you?

🖝 MEET YOUR REAL SELF 🖝

"Blessed art Thou, O Lord our God, who has not made me a woman" (Elizabeth Hill, "Issues," *Jews for Jesus,* vol. 5:3). How would you feel if your pastor spoke the words of this traditional Jewish prayer to God from the pulpit some Sunday morning? To say that your inner temperature would shoot to boiling is probably not to overstate the case.

It's a fact, though, that women I know have been laced with similar verbal blows spoken by self-centered others which, as a result, have scarred their sense of femaleness.

"Why couldn't you have been a boy!"

"How can you be so clumsy? Look how graceful your sister is!"

"I've found someone else. She makes me feel like a real man."

"Move over in bed, Honey. I'll just put your teddy bear on the chair. Don't worry; what I'm doing is just the way a daddy shows his little girl he loves her."

There are the good moments too, when little-girlness and big-girlness was and is a delight. The time we fell in love. The Saturday afternoon we wore satin down the aisle as a bridesmaid.

Perhaps, though, most of the time we hardly think about being female. Maybe it only hits us when we experience PMS (premenstrual syndrome), menstrual cramps, or hot flashes. The rest of the time it's a given, like being 5' 4" or having beauty marks on our arms.

What *do* we think about being female? Do we realize how much circumstances and environment have shaped our perception of what it means? How much the current attitudes of society have affected us?

In my own life span, a woman's stereotype has changed dramatically. From homemakers in housedresses, role models have been transformed into executives in business suits. From a stereotype as "the weaker sex" to liberation until the genders have almost merged. Male and female wear the same hairstyles and clothing, and work at the same jobs.

While some of the changes have been positive and others have not, the point is that what we think about being female, to a large degree, is the result of the kind of information we've taken in. That image is unique to each of us. So each of us has a view of our femaleness that is peculiar to us alone. Of course, we probably didn't sit down one day and consciously decide "This is what it means to be a woman." Like Topsy, it "just growed" unexamined.

"Sexual identity is the image of the self as a male or female and convictions about what membership in that group implies," writes Betty Yorburg (*Sexual Identity*, John Wiley and Sons, p. 1). The key word here is *convictions*. A personal certainty that cuts through the effluvium.

At some point, we must each stop and determine for ourselves what it means to be female. What's more, we must build our findings, not on the shifting social consensus or others' prejudices, but the absolutes of God.

At the core of what He has revealed is this: He created human beings in two genders, not only for sexual purposes, but so both the male and female could be peculiar expressions of His very nature.

"Maleness and femaleness represent spiritual realities that reflect the nature of God and the spiritual universe" (Paul and Jean Bubna, "God Made Them Male and Female," *The Alliance Witness*, April 4, 1980, p. 9). How does God reveal Himself through the female gender?

As giver of life—pictorialized in the hidden formation of a child in the womb of a woman.

As nurturer—It's from her own body that woman nourishes a child at birth. Afterward, she goes on to develop and train the young one out of the desire God implanted in her. In that way, she reflects a facet of the One who created her. And even though we, as individual women, may not be mothers, He gives other opportunities to demonstrate those creative, gentling capacities like His own of nourishing, developing, and training.

As intuitive thinker—Intuition is the ability to know something without consciously reasoning. Recent scientific evidence seems to be showing that women may experience the world in a way that men do not—perhaps because of hormonal differences—and that may even affect their brain. Researchers believe that may be the reason women are different from men in other than the obvious ways. These may include the proverbial "women's intuition," which, in a very limited, human fashion, reveals something of the nature of God.

What better reason to rejoice because we are women than that we have been given the unique opportunity to express something of who God is! Knowing that, we can turn the rabbi's prayer inside out: "Blessed art Thou, O Lord our God, who *has* made me a woman."

❧ *BUILD YOUR OWN IDENTITY* ❧

Continue developing your "Celebrating Who I Am" album.

1. Recall your first menstrual cycle and your first date. Are these pleasant or unpleasant memories? Has anything about these experiences influenced the way you see yourself as a woman?

2. In addition to being an individual woman, you're part of the human race called "womanhood." This week, observe your fellow women in church, at work, while shopping, in your neighborhood. Jot down as many ways that you are alike as you discover. Describe the ways in which this makes you feel closer to other women.

3. Memorize Genesis 1:27. As you study, reflect on the fact that the human race has been created in two genders and that you, as a female, can demonstrate qualities of God like gentleness and nurturing.

4. Each day this week, reflect on one aspect of what it means to be a woman. How does your perception of yourself line up with God's?
   Day 1   Your physical body
   Day 2   Your sexuality
   Day 3   Your marital status
   Day 4   Motherhood, whether your own or that of females in general
   Day 5   Your identity as a "woman"
   Day 6   Your femininity

5. Celebrate your femaleness by soaking extendedly in a hot bath—perhaps even using bubbles. If that's not possible, choose a substitute activity that makes you feel feminine. While you're doing it, appreciate before God the various aspects of womanhood—from physical to spiritual. Write a paragraph that sums up your thoughts and feelings.

 YOUR GIFTEDNESS

❧WHO GOD SAYS YOU ARE ❧

1. What is one of the most cherished gifts you've ever received? Why?

2. Have you ever been given a gift that was an unexpected generosity? What impact did it have on your life?

3. When someone gives you a gift, do you tend to use/display it or save it? Why? What do you learn about gift-giving and receiving from your answers to the above questions?

4. The first man and woman had the ability to do certain things. Which abilities are named or implied in Genesis 1:28; 2:15, 19-20; 3:7, 17-19.

5. These abilities were designed to enable man to live in the natural world. "Talents . . . are gifts on a physical or social level only, given

to benefit mankind in its 'natural life' " (Ray C. Stedman, *Body Life*, Regal Books). What natural ability did Jacob display in Genesis 30:25-30?

6. List three human abilities that a Miss America contestant might demonstrate in the talent competition.

7. In the New Testament, God describes different kinds of abilities. These are ones He bestows on Christians and are discussed in 1 Corinthians 12. How are these specific abilities described in verse 1? From whom do they come? See verses 4-7.

8. The word *gift* comes from the Greek word "charisma" and means a special endowment from God that is an expression of His grace. "Spiritual gifts . . . are given for benefit in the realm of the spirit, the realm of an individual's relationship to God" (Stedman, *Body Life*, Regal Books). How would you explain the difference between a talent and a spiritual gift?

9. What five words come immediately to mind when you think of receiving material gifts? How do they relate to the subject of spiritual gifts as presented in this chapter?

10. First Corinthians 12:7 and Ephesians 4:11-13 explain why God gives Christians spiritual gifts. Look these verses up in several

translations and then write the reason in your own words.

11. To what does the author Paul compare the church (to whom God has given these gifts) in 1 Corinthians 12? What key words in verses 12-14 describe the closeness of Christians to each other? How does being part of a church described like that make you feel?

12. Reread 1 Corinthians 14:26. What principle is stated here about the importance of every Christian's ministry through her gifts? Write a slogan that could be used in a Christian advertisement that sums it up.

13. You are talking with a friend who laments that she doesn't have any such gifts. What answers can you give her from 1 Corinthians 12:7, 11; 14 and Romans 12:6a?

14. Suppose your friend objects that women aren't specifically referred to in this chapter. Which nouns or pronouns such as *man, men,* (meaning mankind), *one another* and *I* are used most often when referring to the human race? Why do you think Paul wrote that way? What would you tell your friend?

15. List as many different spiritual gifts that are mentioned in Romans 12:6-8 and 1 Corinthians 12:28; 14 as you can find. When unsure of a definition, look the word up in the dictionary.

16. In the following passages, list the name of the woman and the gift described. Or describe in general terms what she did.

    Exodus 15:20

    Matthew 27:55-56

    Acts 9:36-43

    Acts 21:9

    Philippians 4:3

    Also list the names of women you can identify in Romans 16:1-16 and a description of their ministry.

17. We go to a gynecologist to care for our female organs, a cardiologist for our heart, and a podiatrist for our feet. Each physician's specialty is important to our body's well-being. What parallel can you draw regarding the ministry of individual women to the well-being of

Christ's spiritual body? What insight does 1 Corinthians 12:14-26 give?

18. While some women suppose they have no spiritual gifts, others are preoccupied with their giftedness. How does Ephesians 4:3 speak to the latter?

19. As Christian women, we are the recipients of God's grace or undeserved kindness. The gifts He gives us are one evidence of that. What do you learn about God's grace from Ephesians 1:7-8; 3:7; 4:7? How is this tied to God's giving of spiritual gifts as a free act out of a loving heart?

20. What advice given by Paul to Timothy in 1 Timothy 4:14 and 2 Timothy 1:6-7 applies to you as well? What particular application of these verses is God making to your life?

21. Ray Stedman points out, "When God chose to visit this earth to demonstrate to mankind the new kind of life he was offering, he did so by incarnating himself. God became flesh and dwelt among us. . . . The life of Jesus is still being manifest among men" (*Body Life*, Regal Books). That means one way He wants to show Himself is through us as we practice the particular spiritual gifts He's given us. Read slowly 1 Peter 4:10, substituting the feminine pronoun *she* for the masculine *he*. Go over it several times, emphasizing each key word or phrase. What commitment would you like to make to God as a result of Peter's message here?

22. Reread questions 1–3 and apply those conclusions about material gifts to spiritual ones. What new thoughts do you have?

🐦 MEET YOUR REAL SELF 🐦

I'd never heard of spiritual gifts the day the Christian education director phoned, asking me to teach juniors in Sunday School. "You don't have to give your answer now."

"Good. I'll pray about it."

A new Christian—and a shy one at that—I was at once excited and terrified at the idea, and terror was my strongest response. Surely God would give me an out.

But only one thing came to me during prayer. *Is there any reason why you shouldn't?* It became immediately clear that fear was *not* a reason.

So, a few Sundays later, there I was, standing in front of 50 or so junior-aged children teaching a lesson about a biblical character I'd never heard of and whose name I could hardly pronounce— Mephibosheth.

My mouth was so dry I felt that with the next word, it would be glued shut. My hands were trembling. But afterward, the superintendent took my hand. "You did a wonderful job and you weren't even nervous."

I was elated. I loved teaching. Everything about the process was fulfilling—from Bible study to presentation (despite my early nervousness). Over the years, in addition to teaching juniors, I taught high school, beginners, primaries, and finally, adults where I more or less settled down.

Along the way, I did learn about spiritual gifts. *Teaching is mine*, I thought with satisfaction. But as a rural missionary, I was confronted with other church positions that went unfilled. Like choir director. So, despite the fact that I didn't have a musical bone in my body, I volunteered.

It was drudgery. I dreaded practice. I especially dreaded performance—standing in front of the congregation leading. It took a while, but I finally had to admit that musicianship was not one of my natural abilities, and certainly not one anointed by God as a way He wanted to minister to the body of Christ through me.

Conducting a choir became a bad memory. So far as I was concerned, teaching was my spiritual gift and I'd be doing that until I was too old to prepare a lesson. But instead, at mid-life I found myself in transition—no longer a missionary, and with less opportunities to teach than I'd had. I was crushed. Why wasn't God using my gift to full advantage?

About that time, I experienced an unmistakable urge to learn to write for publication. That's when I began studying books on writing and practicing whenever I could. After months, I sensed a distinct impression that I should *do it*—write an article and send it to a periodical, and take my chance at being rejected.

Instead of rejection, I received a letter from the editor. "Your article has been accepted for publication." That sale was followed by others. A few years later, God led me to begin writing books as well.

Through my own experience and periodic reexamination of the Scriptures, I've learned some key principles about spiritual gifts.

God will show you what your gifts are. That Christian education director's phone call was the beginning of several beckonings by God to minister in a particular way. God will give us the desire and opportunity, but it's up to us to do the work to see whether or not we do have the ability.

You'll love using your gift. Maybe not at first and maybe not all the time. But frequently, you'll experience a sense of fulfillment that this has come out of your core and is among the most rewarding things you do.

One gift can be used in several ways. In my case, that meant teaching in all kinds of capacities and all kinds of circumstances, but teaching through writing and speaking as well.

You may be multi-gifted. God may anoint your natural ability to draw pictures to minister to the body of Christ. He may anoint your love of people as well. Later, He may use you to heal the emotional wounds of women with whom He puts you in contact.

Don't feel guilty when you honestly don't have time for full-time ministry. Women have come to me frustrated. "I think God has gifted me to write, but I have a full-time job and two small children to care for. I just can't find time."

My answer to such a woman is that, while she may not be able to minister on the scale she'd like, she can do something—perhaps write a poem for her church newsletter. Expect God to minister through you *now*, no matter what stage of life you're in. He will energize you to do so in a way you can manage.

Be sure to let God, not a sense of guilt, direct you. If you don't, you'll find yourself sweating over a job (like choir director!) for which you are not gifted.

Don't stereotype yourself. Let God, not a mental image of what's traditional for women to do, set your course. Pray. Follow your desires. Explore opportunities. Cultivate and refine your natural abilities. Ignore fear of failure. Expect others to confirm.

See your gifts as part of who you are. To know that you're gifted in particular ways does not make you pretentious. For it's God Himself who has chosen to equip each of us in particular ways "so that the body of Christ may be built up" (Ephesians 4:12).

Most importantly, *make living in the Holy Spirit your priority.* Because the gift, the power, and the enthusiasm to incarnate Christ in some small way, comes from Him.

❧ BUILD YOUR OWN IDENTITY ❧

Continue developing your "Celebrating Who I Am" album.

1. Write a description in your album of three times when people have ministered to you through their gifts. Tell how they helped you grow spiritually in some way.

2. Reflect each day on one of the following questions or exercises and write your thoughts.

   ☐ Do you have trouble believing you are spiritually gifted? What does Scripture have to say about that?

   ☐ Has God been urging you to cultivate some ability to use for Him? Does He want you to use some ability you have in a new way? What steps should you take?

   ☐ What questions do you have about your spiritual gifts, and who can you talk to about them?

   ☐ Are you underinvolved in ministering or overinvolved? If either, what changes should you make?

   ☐ What do you believe the area of your giftedness to be? Would you feel comfortable reading what you've just written to others? Why or why not?

   ☐ Are there areas in which your perception of spiritual giftedness needs adjusting to Scripture?

3. Memorize 1 Peter 4:10. As you do, think about the fact that these abilities are given to you by God, are energized by Him, and are to be used to serve others.

4. Ask a mature Christian woman how she discovered what her spiritual abilities are and what she's learned about ministering through the use of them.

5. Celebrate your giftedness by telling at least one woman how she has ministered to you. Ask her how you can pray for her so she may be used more effectively for God.

CHAPTER EIGHT

Celebrate YOUR HUMANITY AND INDIVIDUALITY

🦋 *WHO GOD SAYS YOU ARE* 🦋

1. List three positive qualities about yourself that you'd put in a résumé for a prospective employer.

2. Describe one thing about yourself that you'd rather no one knew. It shouldn't be your worst secret, but something you wish were different about yourself.

3. Compare yourself to a woman friend in the following areas: taste in clothes, hobbies, attitude toward housework, disposition.

4. Imagine that the sixth day of creation was almost over and all life forms from the fifth day on were gathered together for a Creation Celebration. At the outset, God explained to each one what its identity and function was on earth. When He came to Adam and Eve what word would He have used to describe their identity and function? See Genesis 2:7.

5. Adam's name explains his identity in part because in Hebrew it means "red" referring to the ground from which he was formed.

What is your response to the fact that mankind was created from dirt? Read Genesis 2:22. Why does this attitude apply to women as well?

6. One of the words used to describe human beings is *fallible*. Look up the definition in the dictionary. How does that differ from *sin* as it is defined in 1 John 3:4?

7. Write "F" next to the following if it is a result of merely being a human being who doesn't do things perfectly and "S" if it is the result of being a sinner.

Feeling stressed because of PMS
Taking God's name in vain
Turning on the dryer with the cat inside because you didn't know he was there.

Do you have any new thoughts about the difference between being a human and being a sinner? If so, describe them.

8. Eve was just like us in that as a human she had intellect, desires, emotions, and a will. She used her intellect in Genesis 3:2 when she said:

In Genesis 3:6, she used her will when she chose:

Although the passages do not describe the emotion she felt, they imply it. How must she have been feeling in Genesis 3:7, 13? What normal human desire is implied in Genesis 4:1?

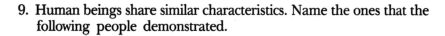
9. Human beings share similar characteristics. Name the ones that the following people demonstrated.

Moses (Exodus 18:13-26)

Mary (Luke 1:28-29)

Peter (John 13:6-9)

The prophets (1 Peter 1:10-11)

What in these passages helps you feel closer to these people?

10. Jesus Christ elevated the status of humans when He Himself became one of us and shared the human experience with us. Next to each passage, write the human characteristic He displayed.

Matthew 26:37-38

Luke 2:40

Luke 4:13

Luke 9:58

John 4:6

Recall a time in your life when you experienced at least two of these. Reflect on Jesus' commonality with you and write your response.

11. At the Creation Celebration described in question four, imagine that God explained to Adam and Eve that each human being would be unique. That's probably easier for us to understand than it would have been for them. Define the word *unique* and describe some things about you that are unlike every other person. One would be your fingerprints.

12. In addition to our physical characteristics, our personal qualities also distinguish us. What personal qualities set the following people apart?

Sarah (Genesis 21:8-10; 1 Peter 3:6)

Elizabeth (Luke 1:5-6; 23-25; 41-45)

Jezebel (1 Kings 21:1-16)

13. Name as many reasons as you can think of why we are each unique. Do they all directly or indirectly come from God? Explain your answer.

14. God chose many diverse people to write portions of Scripture. Why do you think He did that? How could the writings of each of the following be of particular help because of their unique experiences and personalities?

David, a shepherd who became king, committed adultery, and was loved by God.

Solomon, David's son, who became a wealthy, wise king, succumbed to materialism, and finally saw the foolishness of that.

Peter, an impulsive fisherman, became stable and faithful to Christ.

Paul, a devout Jew, persecuted Christians but was born again and thoroughly converted as a follower of Christ.

15. Has the personality, experience, and/or writing of one of these people helped you in a particular way? If so, tell how.

16. What struggle have you had in overcoming a character flaw that might help others?

❦ *MEET YOUR REAL SELF* ❦

"Today? You have an appointment to interview me today?" The young man paused as though thinking back through an internal calendar. "I'm sure I have it down for tomorrow."

I smiled with what I hoped was understanding. *His secretary's error.* But back home when I consulted my calendar, I groaned. Instead of looking at today's appointments, *I'd* been looking at tomorrow's.

When we met the next day and I admitted my error, my voice didn't waver with embarrassment. It's OK, I know now, to make mistakes so long as I learn from them.

I haven't always known that. Making mistakes mortified me. Then God led me through a series of circumstances to change that aspect of my personality. The most prominent was that I had to go to work outside my home. The job God led me to was that of salesclerk.

As I hung my coat in my locker, I trembled with first-day-of-work fear that I'd make some stupid mistake, get caught, and be fired.

And make mistakes I did—regularly. "That's OK," management would assure me. "Everyone does it. That's how we learn." God helped me integrate that truth into my mind. *You are a female human being. A learner.* Often, it's by doing things wrong that we find out how to do things right.

As humans, we are born with certain instincts. We also have an intellect. But it must be fed information and learn behavior through repetition in a fumbling, bumbling process.

One of the most important things we have to learn is who we are. A unique individual, unlike any other.

Perhaps one of the times that fact hits me hardest is when I'm in a crowd. Just yesterday, I was at a conference with about a hundred others, mostly women. As I sat in the auditorium, ahead was Gretchen, who weeps when we sing choruses. Cara was in front of her and spoke her ideas aloud when no one else dared. Fran bit her fingernails. Tess took copious notes while Harriet took none.

While I sensed a bonding to each, I also felt a strong sense of separateness from them. Because of my genes, my experiences, and my life environment, I was someone different from all of them. *I was me.*

I haven't always sensed my particular individuality or been satisfied to live within its framework. Some of my friends are still struggling the same way. Perhaps that's because we women tend to measure ourselves by a Christian female stereotype who has a tinkling voice, is gentle, and everlastingly patient.

Which evangelical assembly line turned out this paper doll? Where did we get the idea that we had to be her? That it wasn't acceptable to be different—to have a booming laugh and a straightforward personality, for example.

After years, and mostly by journaling my thoughts and feelings and lining them up against biblical truth, I have found courage to rip the paper doll from the walls of my mind.

I am me.

I am a woman who likes to wear red.

Who reads in bed and loves caramel nut ice cream.

I love to listen to Dino tapes.

I am not naturally patient; I have had to learn that quality.

My voice is deep, not tinkling. I am not sweet; I see life with a slightly off-kilter sense of humor.

I do not like to climb ladders.

I am overly tenacious and will stay with a project long after it should have been scrapped.

I am a woman for whom intimacy with Jesus Christ is the core of her life.

I am a female human—sixth-day, created creature. So are we all. Stumbling, bumbling learners with the ability to relate to the planet on which we live. We see, feel, touch, taste, smell, think, and choose.

We are individuals—designer models and not off the rack—a fact that stirs within us pure wonder. What marvelous creatures we are. More than that—what an indescribable God Jehovah is.

❧ BUILD YOUR OWN IDENTITY ❧

Continue developing your "Celebrating Who I Am" album.

1. Ask yourself the following questions: Have you tended to get down on yourself from time to time because you struggle with human qualities like exhaustion or emotions like anger? Are such things wrong in themselves? Have you had misconceptions about what it means to be human? What are they and why are they wrong? How do you need to change?

2. Which of these problems—menstrual cramps, PMS, pregnancy problems, postpartum blues, menopause—inherent in human females, have bothered you? How did they affect your disposition? How did you handle the situation? Would you do anything differently?

3. Memorize the one facet of Jesus' humanity from question 10 (*Who God Says You Are*) that seems most important to you. Ask yourself why you chose that one and how you can apply that fact to your own life.

4. Focus on your individuality this week by describing yourself in each of the following ways:
   - ☐ Physically. Describe yourself for someone who is to meet you at the airport but has never seen you.
   - ☐ Intellectually. What are you good at?
   - ☐ Emotionally. Are you restrained or expressive?
   - ☐ Spiritually. What about your relationship with God is most important to you?
   - ☐ Special interests. What are your favorite recreational activities?
   - ☐ Priorities and goals. Would you rather buy a house, take a vacation to Hawaii, or serve as a short-term missionary?

5. Celebrate the fact that you are a unique female human being by creating something that is one of a kind. Choose an area in which you feel adept. Make it your private exclamation of praise because God has created you as one of a kind.

CHAPTER NINE

Celebrate YOUR SPIRITUALITY AND POTENTIAL

❧ *WHO GOD SAYS YOU ARE* ❧

1. If you could physically resemble any person, who would it be? Why?

2. Which member of your family are you most like in personality qualities? Name those qualities.

3. What quality does a family member display that you consider most admirable and would like for yourself? What would you have to do for that to happen?

4. What phrases in Genesis 1:27 and 5:1 describe man's likeness to God—one that separates him from all other created beings?

5. The following passages also name the part of man that is like God. What additional information do you learn?

Proverbs 20:27

Ecclesiastes 12:7

6. In his book, *The Great Doctrines of the Bible* (Moody Press, p. 127), William Evans explains: "*Image* means the shadow or outline of a figure, while *likeness* denotes the resemblance of that shadow to the figure." What further insight into your likeness to God does that give you?

7. The ways in which we are like God aren't physical but moral. In what ways does Paul in Ephesians 4:23-24 say our moral nature can be like God's?

8. Because God is a Spirit and we have a spirit, we can have a relationship with Him that no other creature can. What one word is used in each of the following passages to describe that relationship?

John 10:14

John 17:3

Galatians 4:9a

9. In some translations of Scripture, the word *know* is used to describe sexual intercourse. "And Adam knew Eve his wife; and she conceived, and bare Cain" (Genesis 4:1, KJV). That most intimate physical act is used as an illustration of spiritual intimacy. Take time to think before God about the implications of that comparison. What new dimensions in your spiritual relationship does this make you desire?

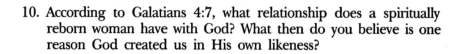
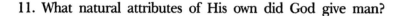

10. According to Galatians 4:7, what relationship does a spiritually reborn woman have with God? What then do you believe is one reason God created us in His own likeness?

11. What natural attributes of His own did God give man?

   Psalm 36:5

   Psalm 116:5

   Isaiah 40:11

   2 Peter 3:9

   1 John 1:9

12. Because we're born with a sinful tendency, we aren't able to consistently reproduce these qualities until we're born again. Read Romans 8:5-15. What person living in the Christian enables her to do so? What must we do to make that possible?

13. Peter describes things we need to know in order to develop a personal, spiritual fitness program in 2 Peter 1:3-8. How do the answers to the following questions help you prepare your own?

   What do we have to store in our mind so we have a clear picture of what God is like? (v. 3)

What has He given us guaranteeing that this change in us can take place? (v. 4)

What specific qualities can we cultivate? (vv. 5-7)

What phrase explains that the change is gradual and not instantaneous? (v. 8)

What is the result of cultivating these qualities? (v. 8)

14. Suppose you were organizing a beauty pageant. What qualities would you consider most important in candidates? What theme song would you choose? What woman would you nominate to be a candidate and why?

15. What name does Paul give to the qualities of God in Galatians 5:22-23? How does John 15:5 say we cultivate them? What does that mean to you?

16. The greater our resemblance to God, the greater our potential to influence society. What word is used repeatedly in Matthew 5:14-16 to illustrate the impact we can have? Reflect on what that word means to you and the insights that gives into the kind of woman God is calling you to be.

17. What further insight do you get from Acts 13:47 and Philippians 2:14-15. Think of specific ways you can live out what it says.

18. Women in Scripture influenced society in particular ways according to the roles they filled. Suppose you were telling a friend who had never heard of them about the importance each had. What would you say?

Huldah, a prophetess who was consulted after the Book of the Law was found and read (2 Kings 22:11-20)

Deborah, a national leader (Judges 4:1-14)

Hannah, a mother who vowed that if God gave her a son, she'd give him to God to serve Him (1 Samuel 3:19-21)

Anna, a widow and prophetess (Luke 2:36-38)

What woman that you've read about in previous lessons would you like to add?

19. What instructions in 2 Timothy 1:6-7 does the Holy Spirit want to apply to your life so that you can realize your potential in the part of the world where you live?

❧ *MEET YOUR REAL SELF* ❧

Spirituality was a word that wagged its finger at me for years. It was a guilt-starter, like Mama's "Be a good girl," when I was growing up.

Such an other-world sound that word had. Accusing, yet at the same time cloud-like and wispy, like eiderdown to gather around oneself and tuck into the crevices of one's soul. To me, it spoke of heavenly deportment and described a woman who glided through the house, always smiling, always unruffled.

Spirituality is the dress all Christian women are to wear, I reasoned. So I set about sewing myself one out of earnest desire.

Not one of the dresses I made (and there were many) covered my nakedness. Finally, tired from trying and failing, I asked the question I should have posed right after my rebirthday: "What *is* spirituality, anyway?"

Using several writers' works, the Holy Spirit helped me understand. The Apostle Paul was one of them. Watchman Nee was another, writing in his book, *The Spiritual Man.*

What I concluded was that spirituality is the outer expression of the inner life in which the spirit of man is united with the Spirit of God.

That posed a second question: "How do I become spiritual?"

The answer? By living in the presence of God obediently moment by moment. By asking for and receiving cleansing continually from a loving Father and not stockpiling guilt. By leaning into God and relinquishing anger or anxiety when some attitude or situation generates it.

God used the years when life for me seemed over (and I had no cloth or energy to sew spiritual dresses) to teach me experientially how to live in union with Him. I was to relax and rest in His presence. Next, I was to own and release the anger and anxiety I felt. Then, I was to choose to go on by leaning into Him and living constructively.

No one was more surprised than I when I began to experience peace rooted in my spirit where God lived; a sense of rightness and strength.

So long as I counted on His strength in me, anxiety and anger, unfanned, gradually died to embers.

In the years that followed, I was to learn that spirituality isn't just the ability to reproduce the qualities of God. It's also learning to have the perspective of God. Paul was speaking of that when he prayed, "That the eyes of your heart may be enlightened" (Ephesians 1:18).

Other Scripture calls that quality "wisdom." There's a growing conviction among women today that job security, advancement, and public recognition isn't what's most important in their lives. Knowing and showing God and seeing events from His point of view is far more valuable.

The tug-of-war between temporal and spiritual wisdom was the same in the first century as it is in ours. Didn't the apostles hunger for power, arguing who would be chief? And didn't Jesus gently take them by their spirits to a better way? "Live by your inside life," He urged them. "See the world from upper story windows."

Perhaps never in American history have women needed to heed His words more. Ideas about who a woman is and who she is to be have exploded. Many of the banners that wave woman's equality are good ones. So are ones that pose her right to an independent identity, the right to develop and use her own abilities, and to influence public thinking, particularly on issues that relate to women.

The fact that we need to burn within, however, is this: what we *do* is not the source of our potential. It's who we *are*.

"You (women) are a chosen people

A royal priesthood

A holy nation

A people belonging to God

That you may declare the praise of Him who called you out of darkness into His wonderful light" (1 Peter 2:9).

We realize our potential by:

☐ being women in whom the Light is on.

☐ being women in whom God is at home.

☐ being chosen, royal, holy women—daughters of God.

☐ using our roles and relationships to demonstrate Christ's qualities, speak from His point of view, and behave as He, the Servant, did.

❧BUILD YOUR OWN IDENTITY❧

Continue developing your "Celebrating Who I Am" album.
1. Write a word description of your Father. Is this the way you've experienced Him to be? Explain your answer.
2. As His daughter, you have the spiritual genes to be like Him. Which of your spiritual features most resemble His? Where do you need the most growth?
3. Memorize 2 Peter 1:3. Instead of the plural pronouns, substitute ones that make it personal. For example: "*Your* divine power has given *me* everything *I* need for life and godliness through *my* knowledge of Him who called *me* by His own glory and goodness" (NIV).
4. Each day this week, reflect on one aspect of your relationship with God:
   ☐ You are indwelled with His Spirit.
   ☐ You have been created to know God intimately.
   ☐ Your new nature has the same moral qualities as your Father's.
   ☐ One reason intimacy with God is difficult for you.
   ☐ Things God is showing you that you can do to improve your relationship.
   ☐ One action you can take to realize your spiritual potential at home or work.
5. Celebrate your spirituality and potential by planning a Father-daughter banquet. The theme will be "In His Image." To emphasize the fact that we can become like our Father, display photographs of daughters and their fathers who resemble one another. Which photos of daughters and their fathers could *you* bring? What songs about your Father could you request? What favorite Bible passage describing your Father could you read? What woman in the Bible could you pantomime because she demonstrated her spiritual potential in her world?

The Bible study you're leading is a celebration. The reason for the festivities is that we are *women*. So each week you'll want to create an upbeat atmosphere. You'll also want to keep in mind the principles that make all Bible studies run smoothly. That means encouraging members to do their study ahead of time and making the group feel comfortable when they're together by being friendly and providing opportunities to get acquainted.

Be sensitive to those less able to find their way around in the Bible. By using the nonthreatening ways to share provided in each lesson, you can draw in the more reticent ones.

Encourage group participation with leading questions like, "What has been your experience?" or "How do you see it?" When discussion gets off track, bring it back and offer to make yourself available after the meeting to anyone with special needs.

Always keep the objective in mind: To see from the Bible who we really are and begin to internalize that identity as our own. To be most helpful, you'll want to honestly evaluate where you are in that process. Then you can guide from your own experience.

Keep reminding them that this is a celebration because, as women, they are unique, valuable, and blessed by God. Choose simple ways suitable to your situation to create a celebratory atmosphere. Use the following to stimulate your thinking: decorations such as balloons, banners, or signs; name tags cut from the funny papers; a graffiti board on which they can write comments weekly; a newsprint mural for drawings about a theme; suitable taped music playing as they arrive.

Most importantly, make it plain that the Holy Spirit is the Teacher. Be in prayer during the week for Him to lead, and open each session with prayer inviting Him to fill that role. Emphasize to the group that the Spirit will continue through the week encouraging each woman to build a biblical image of who she is.

🍂 *LEADER'S GUIDE 1* 🍂

Objective
To help group members see themselves as wondrous creations of God.

Personal Preparation
☐ Complete Session 1.
☐ Think of choruses that focus on key words from Genesis 1–2. Get facts about human reproduction. Work through your own answers to the questions in *Who God Says You Are.*

Group Participation
☐ Have women introduce themselves by using answers from questions 1–3 in *Who God Says You Are.* Discuss which information tells who we really are.
☐ What titles have women given Genesis 1–2? (question 5) Have them read the newspaper headline they wrote in question 9 and give words that describe their feelings (question 8). If appropriate, have the group sing a few choruses that focus on key words and feelings they are reminded of.
☐ Find out how women feel about being called "Adam's rib." Do they feel less of a miraculous creature because they are the result of sexual reproduction? What social factors cause that? Talk about why human reproduction is as miraculous as original creation.
☐ Ask a group member to read Psalm 139:14-16. Discuss the five factors about their own creation they listed in question 14. Ask volunteers to put each in their own words and say what it means to them.
☐ Have women had a problem with the fact that the word *man* is used to refer to both sexes? Discuss factors in questions 15 and 16 that are significant.
☐ Ask women to share their album entries from #1 and their drawings from #4 in *Build Your Own Identity.*
☐ Share party plans from #5 in *Build Your Own Identity.* If the group would like to plan such a party at the end of this study, appoint a committee. Close with brief prayers expressing the group's response to the lesson.

❦ LEADER'S GUIDE 2 ❦

Objective
To see afresh the origin of our sinful state and understand and appreciate God's plan for restoration to fellowship.

Personal Preparation
☐ Complete Session 2.
☐ Outline ideas for a play where the serpent is put on trial. Think through elements of Paul's testimony in 1 Timothy 1:15-16. Make sure the plan of salvation is clearly presented. Prepare through prayer and suggest women with questions talk with you after class. Know how you'd answer other questions.

Group Participation
☐ Share the kind of physical and spiritual make-over you'd like and ask others to do so too.
☐ Ask a volunteer to play the part of the serpent on the witness stand. Have another play the part of the prosecuting attorney and ask questions based on Genesis 2:15-17 and 3:1-6 to show that he lied and seduced Eve. Have one person sum up for the group, who is the jury.
☐ Discuss the elements of Paul's testimony in 1 Timothy 1:15-16. Then ask volunteers to tell about their rebirth experience. How is everyday life different since their rebirth?
☐ Based on questions 22 and 23 (*Who God Says You Are*), have someone share what they'd tell a friend who wanted to understand salvation more completely.
☐ In smaller groups of three or so, have women discuss the author's question: "I was a new creature. Then why wasn't I completely transformed, with shiny, new habits?" Have they ever experienced similar uncertainties? What have they learned? One member of each group could summarize their findings.
☐ As women tell how they'll celebrate their rebirthday (*Build Your Own Identity*, #5), list the date next to each name. Assign each a partner to send a greeting on the other's rebirthday celebration.

♠ LEADER'S GUIDE 3 ♠

Objective
To see our roles as ways to serve God, not ways to gain identity.

Personal Preparation
   ☐ Complete Session 3.
   ☐ Collect ads that represent the media's portrayal of women. Assemble newspaper clippings (*Build Your Own Identity*, #4) for discussion starters. Use principles from *Meet Your Real Self* to stimulate discussion for all questions.

Group Participation
   ☐ Discuss the image of women in ads you've collected. Ask: **What stereotypes about women does media portray—especially regarding work? How does that influence your thinking?**
   ☐ As a group, explore mankind's dominion over the earth from Genesis 1:26 and sin's effect. Refer to the newspaper clippings and ask women to share their reflections from *Build Your Own Identity*, #4 about ways women can participate in that responsibility.
   ☐ Read Hannah's story from 1 Samuel 1:1-20. Then ask one woman to tell it as though it were her own. Say: **Suppose Hannah were your friend. What would you have told her when she was barren?**
   ☐ In two minutes, have women list all the roles they fill. Give them time to review *Meet Your Real Self*, then talk about the temptation to identify ourselves by our roles. Ask what principles in that segment seem significant to them.
   ☐ Carry the discussion further in groups of twos using the questions in *Build Your Own Identity*, #3. Pray for one another.
   ☐ As a group, brainstorm practical ways you can put Ephesians 6:7-8 in practice, serving God through responsibilities.
   ☐ Refer to *Build Your Own Identity*, #5 and ask: **What persons will you write or call? What will you say?**

🍂 *LEADER'S GUIDE 4* 🍂

Objective
To internalize the fact that we are highly prized by God and are to view ourselves through His eyes.

Personal Preparation
□ Complete Session 4.
□ Be ready to read Ephesians 1:2-14, substituting personal pronouns. Review five ways of internalizing our identity. Think through answers for the questions below.

Group Participation
□ Ask women to describe one item that's most valuable to them and why. Have the group come up with a list of top reasons why we prize things, besides their dollar value.
□ Now have women brainstorm a list of reasons why God values us and ways He's shown and told us that.
□ Read Ephesians 1:1-14 to the group, substituting personal pronouns, as they sit with eyes closed. Then go over answers to question 14 in *Who God Says You Are*. In groups of two, have women alternate reading those statements to one another as though God Himself were speaking, so they're viewing themselves through His eyes.
□ Give time to review *Meet Your Real Self*. Ask women to draw a picture describing a scene of their own when they devalued themselves and a sentence or two of explanation. Be sure they do not sign the drawing. After sharing pictures with the group, discuss the five ways of internalizing their biblical identity from *Meet Your Real Self* that have worked for them.
□ Say: **Women who value themselves take care of themselves. What are some practical ways we can do that?**
□ Encourage volunteers to read the letters they wrote to God regarding their worth (*Build Your Own Identity*, #5). Close with sentence prayers of praise.

❧ *LEADER'S GUIDE 5* ❧

Objective
To internalize the fact of God's love and consider ways to make it real in women's lives.

Personal Preparation
   ☐ Complete Session 5.
   ☐ Be ready with your own answers to each of the questions so you can contribute to and stimulate discussion.

Group Participation
   ☐ Review the definition of agape love (*Meet Your Real Self,* #5). Ask women to share answers to questions 1–4 (*Who God Says You Are*). Talk about the positive impact of being loved and the negative impact of love withheld.
   ☐ Questions 6, 7, 9, 11, 12, 13, 15, and 17 (*Who God Says You Are*) describe ways we can know that God loves us. Divide into small groups and assign one question to each group. Use as many questions as you choose. Ask groups to use information they glean to complete the following sentence, which one of them will read to the class: "I want you to know today that God loves you. You can know that because. . . . "
   ☐ Give women time to review *Meet Your Real Self.* Brainstorm reasons why it's sometimes hard to believe in God's love. Discuss solutions given and others they think of.
   ☐ Ask: **How has God demonstrated agape love recently through an answered prayer? How can we help one another believe in God's love?**
   ☐ Read Psalm 136:1-9 responsively. Give women an opportunity to read the alternate lines they've written (*Build Your Own Identity,* #4). Close by singing favorite choruses about God's love. Ask women one way they'd like to grow in the knowledge of God's love. Pray for one another.

🍃 *LEADER'S GUIDE 6* 🍃

Objective
To form a personal concept from a scriptural point of view of what it means to be female.

Personal Preparation
  ☐ Complete Session 6.
  ☐ Have newsprint or other material for question 3 (*Who God Says You Are*) and ideas to guide the discussion. Work through each question so you'll be able to guide the group in thinking and forming conclusions.

Group Participation
  ☐ Brainstorm definitions of *female* and *woman* and come up with one or two sentences summarizing each.
  ☐ Divide into small groups and give three minutes to list "What we like about being a woman," and three minutes to list "What we don't like about being a woman." Come together and discuss lists and perceptions of femaleness.
  ☐ List the following aspects of being a woman on newsprint: sexuality, helper, equality, marital status, submission. Ask: **What is God's point of view on each?** Refer to Scripture passages in *Who God Says You Are* when necessary. Then discuss the wrong thinking about each that is prevalent in our society. Put together one or two sentences summarizing the biblical view of each aspect.
  ☐ Give time to review *Meet Your Real Self*, then ask what they think the main reasons are that women have trouble forming a positive identity as females. Ask for their thoughts on the fact that God revealed Himself in two genders so each could be peculiar expressions of His nature.
  ☐ Ask what they'd do to celebrate their femininity. Give them time to imagine they're doing it now. What are they thinking and feeling? Close in group prayer in which they reflect to God on their womanhood.

🍃 *LEADER'S GUIDE 7* 🍃

Objective
To enable women to see that they are gifted and that spiritual gifts are God's way of enabling His body to be effective.

Personal Preparation
  ☐ Complete Session 7.
  ☐ Think through answers to all questions. Write brief scenarios of a woman who can't believe she's gifted and one who is afraid to use her gifts. Have a wrapped package ready.

Group Participation
  ☐ Ask several women to share answers to questions 1–3 (*Who God Says You Are*), including what they have learned about giftedness.
  ☐ Review definitions of natural ability and spiritual gifts. Brainstorm natural abilities that can be used to serve God and their experiences in doing so.
  ☐ Have volunteers read Romans 12:4-8 and 1 Corinthians 12. Guide members to find verses that describe the source of gifts, reason for, the value of all gifts, and the fact that all are gifted. Put together a list of gifts and definitions of each.
  ☐ Vote on the best advertising slogan (*Who God Says You Are*, question 12), keeping in mind the main point of the Scripture it is to embody and the desired result.
  ☐ Read the scenarios you have prepared and ask the group to respond compassionately according to scriptural principles.
  ☐ Encourage women to describe those who influenced their lives through the use of their gifts, and one reason those persons are role models.
  ☐ Celebrate by passing around a wrapped package, explaining that it is symbolic of God's gifts and have members tell one another, "You are gifted too." Use #2 in *Build Your Own Identity* to explore their responses, incorporating the principles in *Meet Your Real Self* as guidelines.

❧ LEADER'S GUIDE 8 ❧

Objective
To encourage women to accept their humanity and see themselves as
unique individuals.

Personal Preparation
☐ Complete Session 8.
☐ Think through answers to each of the following questions. Put
together a list of uniqueness in natural creation such as fingerprints and
voiceprints.

Group Participation
☐ Allow each member one minute to talk with a neighbor about her
positive qualities and one minute to talk about negative ones. Which was
easier and why? What insight do we gain?
☐ Review definitions of *human* and *sinful*. Have they confused the
two? Refer to the author's experiences in *Meet Your Real Self* and *Build
Your Own Identity*, #1–2.
☐ Discuss human characteristics and how they were demonstrated in
Eve's life (*Who God Says You Are*, question 8). Ask women to write a
paragraph that begins "Because I am a human being . . . " and discuss
what they've written.
☐ List human characteristics Jesus displayed (*Who s-2od Says You Are*,
question 10). Using *Build Your Own Identity*, #3, talk about how the fact
that He was human helps us accept our humanness.
☐ Talk about uniqueness in natural creation as well as our physical
bodies. What conclusions do we draw about God?
☐ Examine the example, "*I am me*. . . . " (*Meet Your Real Self*) and
#4 (*Build Your Own Identity*). Then have members make their own lists
describing themselves as unique. Ask them to share in groups of two.
☐ Celebrate by sharing answers to #5 (*Build Your Own Identity*).

❧ *LEADER'S GUIDE 9* ❧

Objective
To understand a woman's spiritual dimension and how to cultivate spirituality and become an influence in our world.

Personal Preparation
☐ Complete Session 9.
☐ Be prepared to stimulate discussion for the questions in this guide.

Group Participation
☐ Have women draw a picture of themselves showing their intellect, emotions, will, and spirit and write one sentence explaining the function of their spirits. Collect, read sentences and discuss.

☐ Ask students to write their responses when they hear each of the following: I am created in God's image; I can *know* God; I am a daughter of God; I can resemble my Father. Share answers aloud and Scriptures from *Who God Says You Are* that add new ideas.

☐ Ask women to complete this sentence: **I want to be more spiritual, but. . . .** Using *Meet Your Real Self* as a guide, define *spiritual* and discuss how to complete this sentence: **One way I can become more spiritual is. . . .**

☐ Review question 12 in *Who God Says You Are*. Define *death* as "separation" and ask: **How can we live out Romans 8:13 during an ordinary day?**

☐ Ask: **How would women like to improve their spiritual fitness program?** (*Who God Says You Are*, question 13) Have a problem-solving session.

☐ Have volunteers describe their beauty pageant from question 14. What do women conclude about beauty?

☐ Write on newsprint: "How can an ordinary woman influence society?" List and discuss answers.

☐ Ask: **What new reasons do you have to celebrate who you are?** Be ready with one way to do that now and decide if the group wants to have a class or other kind of party. Use festivity ideas from each lesson and consult your committee if you appointed one in session 1.